Explore and Draw

Dinosaurs

Ann Becker

www.rourkepublishing.com

Editor: Penny Dowdy
Art Direction: Tarang Saggar (Q2AMedia)
Designers: Shruti Aggarwal, Jaspreet Singh (Q2AMedia)
Picture researcher: Farheen Aadil (Q2AMedia)
Picture credits:
t=top b=bottom c=centre l=left r=right

Cover: John E Marriott/All Canada Photo/Photolibrary,
Stephen Coburn/Shutterstock, Juliengrondin/Shutterstock.
Insides: Martin1985/Dreamstime: 6, Andreas Meyer/Shutterstock: 7,
Relison/Bigstockphoto: 10, Dea Picture Library: 11,
Oxford Scientific/Jupiterimages: 14, Dea Picture Library: 15,
Andreas Meyer/123rf: 18, Dea Picture Library: 19.
Q2AMedia Art Bank: Cover, Title Page, 4, 5, 8, 9, 12, 13, 16, 17, 20, 21.

Library of Congress Cataloging-in-Publication Data

Becker, Ann, 1965 Oct. 6-
Dinosaurs : explore and draw / Ann Becker.
p. cm. – (Explore and draw)
Includes index.
ISBN 978-1-60694-350-2 (hard cover)
ISBN 978-1-60694-834-7 (soft cover)
1. Dinosaurs in art–Juvenile literature. 2. Drawing–Technique–Juvenile literature.
I. Title. II. Title: Explore and draw.
NC780.5.B43 2009
743.6–dc22
2009021612

Printed in the USA
CG/CG

www.rourkepublishing.com - rourke@rourkepublishing.com
Post Office Box 643328 Vero Beach, Florida 32964

Contents

Technique

Before you start drawing dinosaurs, let's talk about space. **Positive space** is the part of your drawing that contains the subject of your drawing. **Negative space** is the space not containing your subject. Drawing the negative space helps you see the shapes of objects and their surroundings.

This drawing shows the positive space. The lines and shading shows off the subject and objects in the drawing.

The lines and shading here show negative space.

Theropods

A giant, sharp-toothed beast bursts out of the jungle! It runs on its hind legs, chasing animals for food. These terrifying dinosaurs were called theropods.

Giant Meat Eaters

Most theropods were **carnivores**. This means that their diet was meat from animals they hunted. As hunters, they were larger and stronger than almost any other creature. Tyrannosaurus rex is the most famous theropod of all.

You can tell this is a carnivore because of its sharp teeth.

Powerful Hind Legs

Theropods had legs in front and back, but they were very different from each other. They stood up on large, strong hind legs. These legs were perfect for running after prey. Their front legs were small, almost like arms. They were probably used to grab things.

Hollow Bones and Feathers

One of the strangest facts about theropods is that the inside of their bones were hollow. But the bones were still strong enough to hold their weight! Another strange fact: a few of these dinosaurs had feathers. The feathers can be seen in fossils. Scientists don't think the feathers were used to fly. But some think that these dinosaurs **evolved** into the birds we know today.

A theropod's back legs were very muscular.

Draw a Tyrannosaurus

Use positive and negative space to draw a T-rex in its environment.

1 Draw a faint line to separate the positive and negative space.

2 Create shading in the negative space. Carefully work around the outline.

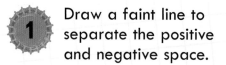

3 Use different shading lines to show plants and hills in the distance.

4 Now add details to the positive space. Don't forget the rocks and ground!

5 Add your final details to the dinosaur. Look how detailed the drawing is all around!

Sauropods

Huge elephants can't compete with the sauropods in size. These giant dinosaurs were the biggest land animals that ever lived. They were over twenty times bigger than the elephants of today!

Plant Eaters

Sauropods were **herbivores**. This means that their whole diet was plants. They had to eat an enormous amount of grass, leaves, and other plants every day. Their bodies were not good at digesting foods, so they ate stones to help break down food in their stomach.

Sauropods had long necks that could reach leaves on the very tops of trees.

What Did They Look Like?

Many of the sauropods looked similar to each other. They walked on long, strong legs that could hold their weight. They had long necks, so they could reach into the highest trees. Some of them held their heads close to the ground. But others walked with their heads lifted up. Many of them had long tails that they could crack like a whip! They also had nostrils that were high up on their heads, not at the end of the snout.

All Over the World

The sauropods were a very successful group of dinosaurs. Their fossils have been found on every continent, except for Antarctica. They learned how to **adapt** to nearly all environments.

This long tail could drive off attacks from other creatures.

Draw an Apatosaurus

An apatosaurus is a sauropod with a thick neck and tail.

1 Separate the positive and negative space with a faint line.

2 Start by drawing some shading in the negative space.

3 What details do you want in the negative space? Add them here.

4 Now start adding lines to the positive space. The dinosaur, the ground, and the rocks in the foreground are part of the positive space.

5 Add your final details to finish your picture.

Ornithopods

What walks on two legs, has a beak, three toes, and lived over seventy million years ago? It wasn't a bird. It was a kind of dinosaur called an **ornithopod.**

Do you notice how the head looks like a bird?

Kind of Like Birds, But Not Exactly

Ornithopods get their name from a Greek phrase that means *bird feet*. Most of them had three toes on their feet. These dinosaurs ran on two back legs, but walked on all four. Like the theropods, their strong back legs were much longer than the ones in front. Because of this, their hips were also very similar to birds of today. Many of them also developed a large beak on the end of the snout.

Strange Heads

Others had a duck-billed head. A lot of them had a large hole in their jaw. But scientists haven't figured out what the purpose of the hole was. They didn't evolve into birds, though. Ornithopods became **extinct** about sixty-five million years ago.

Grazing Dinosaurs

Like a lot of dinosaurs, ornithopods were herbivores. On four legs, they grazed on low-growing plants. The earliest ornithopods were only about three feet (about one meter) long. But some grew to over fifteen feet (4.6 meters). They were very successful in adapting to different places. Their fossils have been found in many places, but most of them lived in North America.

This ornithopod looks more like today's lizards than birds.

Draw the Iguanodon

An iguanadon was a large plant-eating ornithopod.

1 Remember to separate the positive and negative space.

2 Shade the negative space. Try light and dark lines to see which you like better.

3 Now add the shapes and textures to the negative space.

4 Add lines and details to the iguanadon.

5 Include details like texture to the skin and dirt on the ground.

Ceratopsians

The heads of **ceratopsians** made them look like armored tanks. And they were just as big as tanks! Even meat eaters didn't want to mess with them.

What Made a Ceratopsian So Different?

Ceratops means *horn-faced*, and that's an excellent description of these dinosaurs. All of them had one or more horns sticking out of their heads.

They also had a hard plate of bone, or a frill behind their heads. Scientists are not sure what the frill was used for. It might have protected the dinosaur's neck, or helped its body get rid of heat. Because of their shorter legs, they probably didn't move as fast as other dinosaurs.

This dinosaur has one horn and a flat plate behind its head.

Plant Eater

The ceratops also had a huge beak and powerful jaw muscles. You might think that these dinosaurs must be meat eaters. But they lived only on plants, grazing close to the ground. Many times, scientists have found several ceratops fossils in the same spot. Based on this, they think that ceratops traveled together in herds.

Where Did They Live?

Most ceratops fossils have been found in Asia. A lot of these finds have been in China and Mongolia. After millions of years, the dinosaurs also **migrated** to North America. Their remains have been discovered in the western United States.

The horns made ceratopsians fierce fighters.

Draw a Triceratops

Tri– means three. The triceratops had three horns.

1. Start with the faint line that separates the positive and negative space.

2. Place some shading in the negative space.

3 Remember that shapes and textures make the negative space more interesting.

4 Add lines to the triceratops body. Notice the design on its frill.

5 Finish with details and shading to make the dinosaur realistic.

Glossary

adapt (uh-DAPT): to change to fit a new situation

carnivores (KAR-nuh-vors): creatures that eat meat

evolved (i-VOLVD): to change over time

extinct (ek-STINGKT): no longer existing

herbivores (HUR-buh-vors): creatures that eat plants

migrated (MYE-grate-id): moved from one place to another with a change of seasons

negative space (NEG-uh-tiv SPAYSS): the space behind and around the subject of a drawing

positive space (POS-uh-tiv SPAYSS): the space taken up by the subject of a drawing

Index

Websites

www.kidsdinos.com/
A website for kids who love dinosaurs.

www.ucmp.berkeley.edu/diapsids/dinosaur.html
A website from the University of California at Berkeley that discusses myths about dinosaurs.

www.fieldmuseum.org/sue/index.html
A website for kids who love dinosaurs.

www.kidsart.com/HotLnk.html
A website that provides links to art websites, supplies, and artists.

http://www.livescience.com/dinosaurs/
A website filled with articles and images devoted to dinosaurs.

http://pubs.usgs.gov/gip/dinosaurs/
A U.S. Geological Service article describing facts and fiction related to dinosaurs.

About the Author
Ann Becker is an avid reader. Ann likes to read books, magazines, and even Internet articles. She hopes that someday she will get to go on a game show and put all of that reading to good use!

About the Illustrator
Maria Menon has been illustrating children's books for almost a decade. She loves making illustrations of animals, especially dragons and dinosaurs. She is fond of pets and has two dogs named Spot and Lara. When she is not busy illustrating, Maria spends her time watching animated movies.